Vera D. Petersen * 1960

THE ATOMIC SUBMARINE

A Practice Combat Patrol

Under the Sea

by Russell Hoban

Author of WHAT DOES IT DO AND HOW DOES IT WORK?

HARPER & BROTHERS   PUBLISHERS   NEW YORK

ACKNOWLEDGMENTS

The author thanks the gentlemen of the United States Navy and the Electric Boat Division of General Dynamics Corporation whose help made this book possible:

FRANK PACE, President of General Dynamics Corporation

COMMANDER WILLIAM BEHRENS, of *Skipjack*

LIEUTENANT ROBERT CONOLLY, of *Skipjack*

CHIEF ENGINEMAN JOHN MORRISSEY, of *Skipjack*

LIEUTENANT RICHARD HOOVER, Public Information Office, U.S.N.

LIEUTENANT ROY INGRAHAM, Public Information Office, U.S.N.

FRANK ANDERSON, Submarine Library, Electric Boat Division

The drawings on pages 6, 7 and 31 are copied from a diagram and photograph provided by the Electric Boat Division of General Dynamics Corporation.

THE ATOMIC SUBMARINE

This book is dedicated to
the brave men and good fellows
of the United States Submarine Force.

Before the use of atomic power, submarines ran on diesel power when they were on the surface. When they were underwater they could not use the diesel engine because it needed too much air.

These submarines ran on batteries when they were underwater. If the submarines went fast the batteries were used up quickly, and even at slow speeds the batteries lasted no longer than thirty-six hours. At the end of that time the submarines had to surface to recharge the batteries.

Because much of their long distance traveling was done on the surface, they were designed to make their best speed there, and they were slower underwater. The diesel engines needed diesel oil, which was carried in the submarine's fuel tanks, and the submarines could not travel long distances without stopping for more fuel.

These submarines could not go far enough or fast enough, or stay underwater long enough, to give our navy the power it needs in these times. The atomic submarine gives us this power.

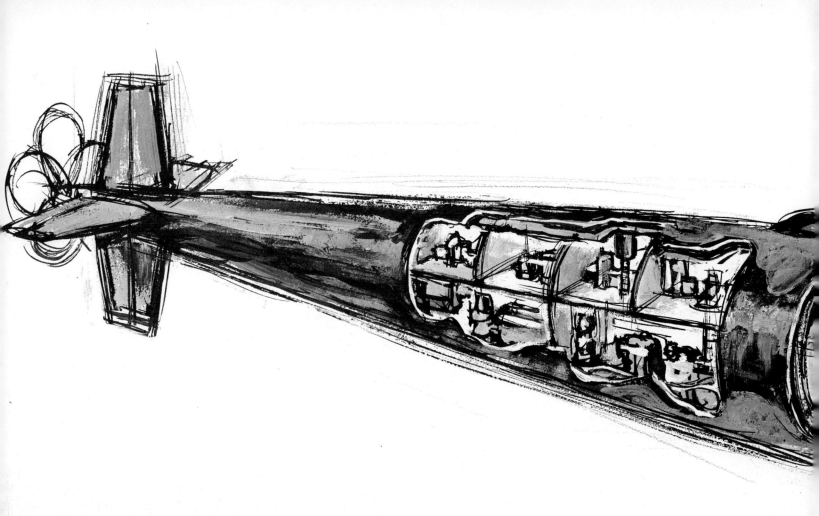

This is an atomic submarine. It is shaped like the whales that swim fast and far, deep under the water. Because atomic power makes it go, it is different from any submarine that was ever made before. The atomic power plant and the shape of the submarine make it go much faster than ordinary submarines, and faster than most surface ships.

The atomic submarine is faster underwater than it is on the surface. Unlike the diesel engine, the atomic reactor needs no air and can be used both on the surface and under water. It can make the submarine go, without stopping, for as long as the fuel lasts. The amount of uranium fuel that the submarine needs to travel underwater for thousands and thousands of miles is so small that it could be carried in your pocket.

The submarine can go fast and far under the sea, and it can stay under as long as it has to. For these reasons the atomic submarine is called the first true submersible.

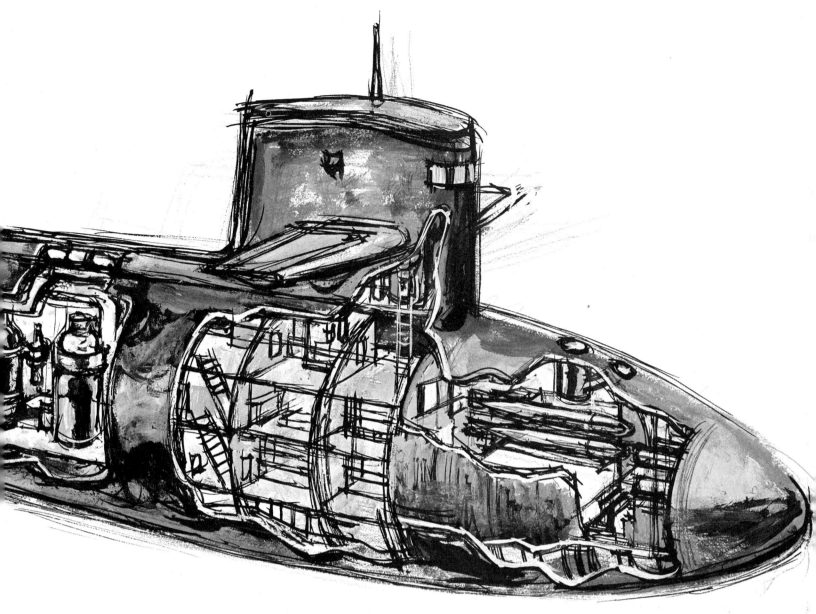

The atomic reactor heats the water that makes the steam that turns the turbines that spin the propeller to make the submarine go. There are oxygen generators to make air for the crew to breathe, and machines to keep the air fresh. There are evaporators to make fresh water from salt water.

Although the submarine is full of the machinery and equipment that make it an undersea fighting ship, every inch of space is figured out carefully, so there is space for bunks to sleep in and lockers for clothes, space for food and space for a galley to cook it in. There is space for spare parts and for tools to fix anything that breaks down.

The atomic submarine has everything it needs to stay under for months at a time and to travel thousands of miles under the sea.

The submarine is cruising 100 feet below the surface when the command comes from the diving officer:

"Make your depth 250 feet."

"Depth 250 feet, sir," comes the reply.

The submarine has an inner hull called the pressure hull in which the men live, and an outer hull in which are ballast tanks. When the submarine first went below the surface, sea water was taken into these tanks, to make the submarine heavy enough to go down. Now the diving planes are tilted to take the submarine down to 250 feet. When the submarine has to come up, compressed air will blow the water out of the tanks so the submarine will be light enough to rise.

There are two men at the controls, working the rudder and the diving planes. This submarine can dive and turn so fast that steering it is like driving an airplane under water.

"Right 15 degrees rudder. Come right to course 045. Steady on course 045."

"Steady on 045, sir."

The submarine will stay on this course for some time, so the automatic pilot and depth controls are set, and the submarine steers itself, hour after hour, on course 045.

The men and ships of our fleet must always be ready for action, and they keep prepared by practicing in naval exercises in which some of the ships and airplanes and submarines take the part of an enemy fleet.

This submarine is on a practice combat patrol with orders to seek out and destroy the enemy. Now the captain gives the command to go up close to the surface, to antenna depth, so the radar antenna can be used.

The water was calm 250 feet down, but close to the surface the submarine pitches and rolls for there is a heavy sea running.

The captain comes into the attack center for a look at the radar repeater.

"Anything yet?"

"No, sir. Nothing yet."

"Take her down again," orders the captain.

In the engine room the engineer on watch looks at everything to make sure it is working just right. If the atomic reactor must be shut down for repairs or inspection, the atomic submarine has other kinds of power that can be used to turn the propeller. It can run on its diesel engine or its batteries or turbo generators.

There is always oil in the engine room sloshing around in the bilges under the floor. If that oil were to be pumped out with the bilge water, it would rise to the surface and show the enemy where the submarine is. So, when the bilges are pumped out, this oil is trapped in tanks in the outer hull as the submarine goes on its secret way deep under the water.

There are men on duty day and night, so there is always a cook in the galley who makes sure that there is plenty of good food for them.

The galley is small, but the cook has the finest equipment for his work. Everything in the galley, from the oven to the mixing machine, is run by electricity from the submarine's generator. The generator is turned by a turbine that is driven by the steam from the water heated by the atomic reactor.

There is a small tube in the galley that is like a torpedo tube. If garbage floated to the surface it would show the enemy where the submarine is. So it is put into plastic bags, weighted with bricks, and ejected from the tube so that it will sink to the bottom.

Some of the men who are off watch are playing cards in the crew's mess. Every submarine has a big box of all kinds of games, but they are not used much because the submariners like to play acey-deucy and cribbage best.

A submarine must find its way in all weathers, and the men inside it must know when an enemy is near. There are many electronic devices on the atomic submarine for this. There are radar and radio and loran for use when running at antenna depth near the surface, and even television is used for navigation under polar ice.

But when the submarine is cruising 250 feet down on a combat patrol and an enemy may be near, sonar is the most important. In his little room that is full of knobs and dials, there is a sonar operator on watch, night and day, always listening for the enemy. His earphones are connected to a hydrophone on the outside of the hull and he listens for sounds in the water. He hears the noises of the whales and the fish nobody sees, and he waits and listens for the enemy. Night and day.

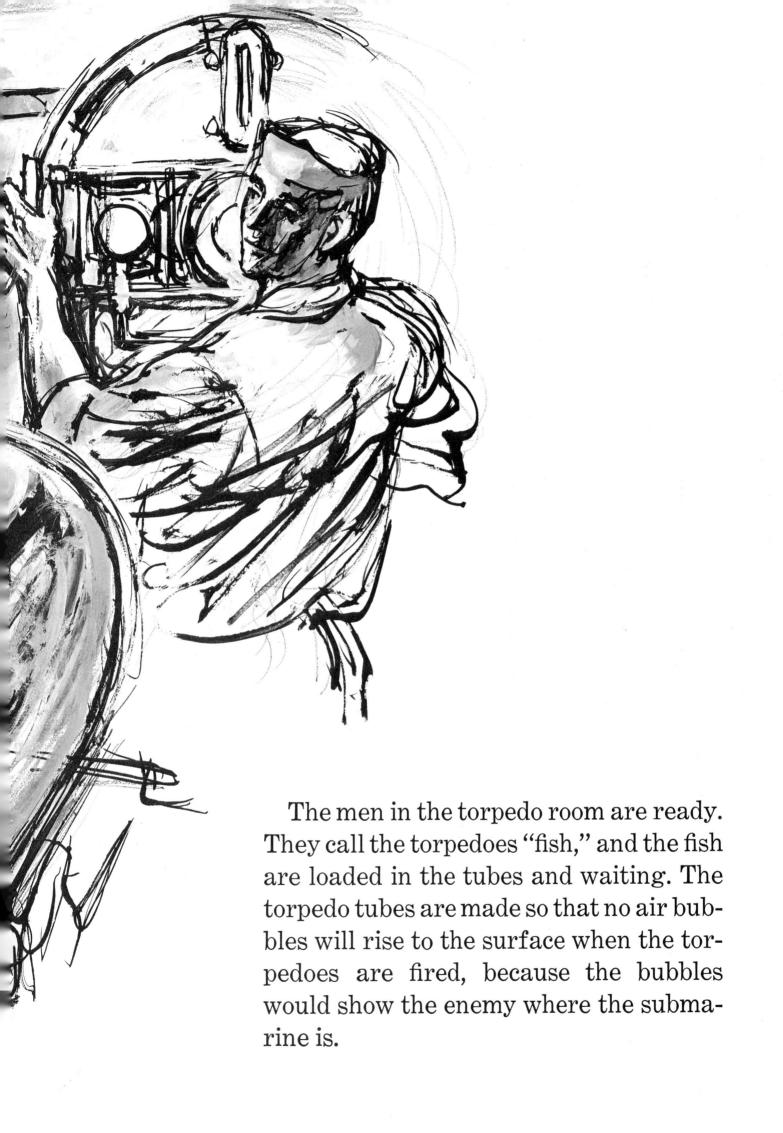

The men in the torpedo room are ready. They call the torpedoes "fish," and the fish are loaded in the tubes and waiting. The torpedo tubes are made so that no air bubbles will rise to the surface when the torpedoes are fired, because the bubbles would show the enemy where the submarine is.

The sonar operator looks up. He hears the beat of propellers underwater. It may be an enemy submarine.

"Possible contact bearing 032 degrees!"

The captain's voice is heard over the announcing system:

"Rig for ultraquiet!"

All unnecessary machinery is shut down. Everything is quiet as the sonar operator listens. Everyone gets ready for action, and phones are manned in every part of the ship.

The sonar operator reports again:

"Contact evaluated as submarine.

"Range 15,000 yards.

"Approximate course 040 degrees.

"Approximate speed 10 knots."

Again the captain's voice.

"Secure from ultraquiet." Absolute silence is no longer required. The men go into action.

"Man battle stations torpedo!"

The general alarm sounds. BONG! BONG! BONG! BONG! BONG!

The men are all at their battle stations and the attack center fills up with people as the range, bearing, course, and speed of the enemy submarine are plotted on the electronic computers. Of course, the submarine is one of our own, but today a practice attack will be carried out as if the submarine were an enemy.

The captain gives his orders:

"We will fire three units. Set speed high. Depth 50 feet."

"Speed high—depth 50 feet!" comes the reply.

"Make ready tubes 1, 2, and 3. Open outer doors."

From the torpedo room:

"Tubes 1, 2, and 3 ready in all respects. Outer doors open!"

The captain orders:

"Shoot on next bearing!"

The sonar operator signals as he gets the bearing. BUZZ! BUZZ!

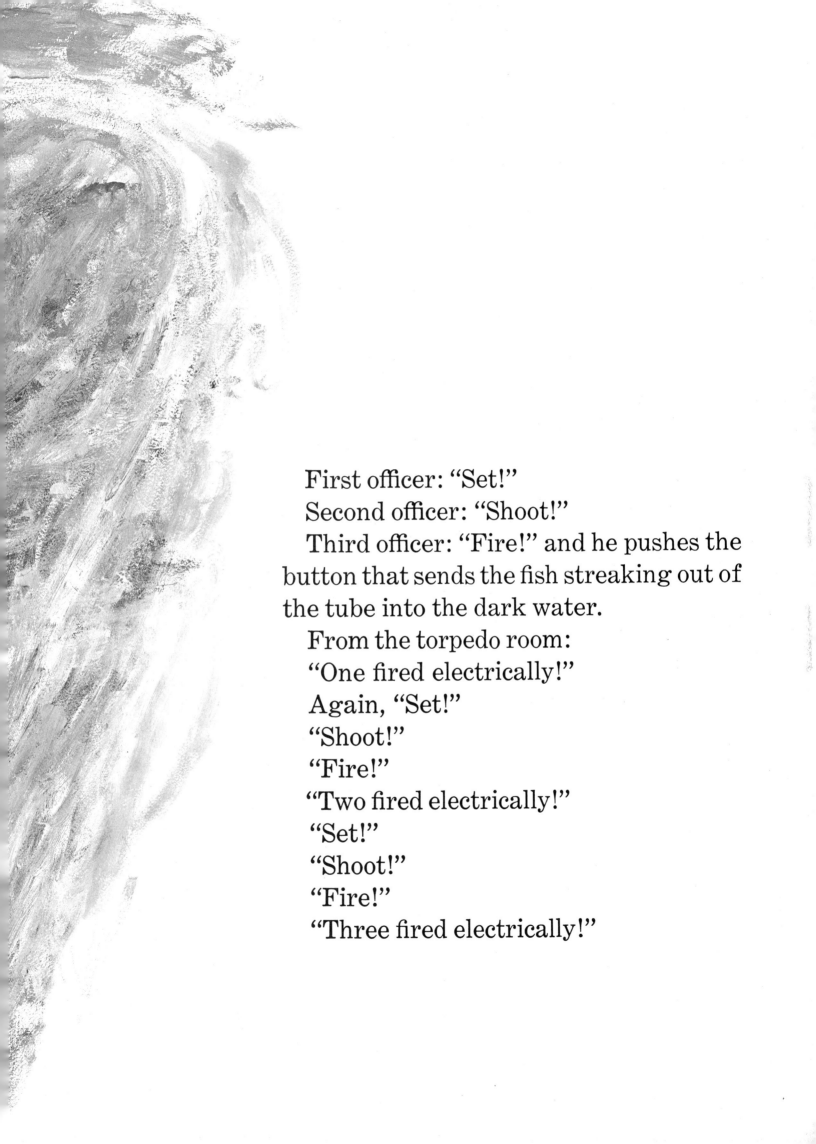

First officer: "Set!"

Second officer: "Shoot!"

Third officer: "Fire!" and he pushes the button that sends the fish streaking out of the tube into the dark water.

From the torpedo room:

"One fired electrically!"

Again, "Set!"

"Shoot!"

"Fire!"

"Two fired electrically!"

"Set!"

"Shoot!"

"Fire!"

"Three fired electrically!"

"Commence reload forward!"

"Commencing reload forward, sir!" The outer doors are shut, the water is drained from the tubes, and the inner doors open. The hydraulic lift, called the "grease rack," comes up with another fish. A hydraulic loader, called a "rabbit," rams the fish into the tube.

In the attack center they listen and wait. The captain and the officers look at their stop watches.

There are two periscopes in the attack center, and when the submarine comes up close to the surface the captain can use a periscope to look around. But now the captain knows that there must be enemy ships and planes around him and his submarine would be seen if it came up. So the submarine stays down, guided in its attack by sonar.

"The first torpedo should be at the target," says the captain.

In a real attack there would be a thunderous WHUMP! fifty feet below the surface and an explosion like this, boiling up in white foam and spray as each torpedo struck the enemy submarine.

Because this is a practice exercise with one of our own submarines acting the part of the enemy, there is no big explosion. Practice torpedoes with plaster heads that shatter when they hit are used. These torpedoes contain just enough explosive to make a noise that will tell the sonar man in the attacking submarine that they have hit the target.

Two of the three torpedoes are direct hits. The practice attack is successful.

The naval exercises are over. The officers and men of the atomic submarine have worked smoothly together as a team. They have tested their ship and themselves, and they have done well. Finally the atomic submarine steams proudly up the river to its base, and the men are home again.